S0-BNE-379

JOB
INTERVIEW
made
EASY

Brian Wilkinson

JUN 28 2011

Limit of Liability/Disclaimer of Warranty: While the publisher and the author have used their best efforts in preparing this book, they make no representations or warranties with respect to the accuracy or completeness of the content of this book and specifically disclaim any implied warranties of merchantability or fitness for a particular purpose. No warranty may be created or extended by sales representatives or written sales materials. You should consult with a professional where appropriate. Neither the publisher nor the author shall be liable for any loss of profit or any other commercial damages, including but not limited to special, incidental, consequential, or other damages.

For general information on our products and services, please contact us on prodinnova@mail.com

Printed in United States.

ISBN : 9782917260043

10 9 8 7 6 5 4 3 2 1

JOB INTERVIEW made EASY

Brian Wilkinson

Congratulations, your resume and your cover letter have succeeded in getting the attention of the recruiter and you have obtained an appointment for a job interview. Know that you have successfully passed the first stage of the recruitment selection process, the same stage in which many candidates have probably failed. Know also that you are not the only one and that there are certainly other candidates that have reached this stage too. However, as there is probably only one job opening, the most difficult is yet to come. What you need to pass with success is called the job interview. While it could be a true nightmare, it is the final step that separates you from a career. But not only from a career, it is the final step that separates you from a business card with a nice title that would allow you to get the most beautiful girls on the block, good medical insurance, and even a company car. Soon, you will forget about your miserable economy class flights because you will be travelling business and probably upgraded to first. Soon, you will be using the word "global" in each phrase that comes of your mouth. But first of all, you have to succeed in that interview and you probably won't have a second chance.

It is literally a liar poker game. Indeed, if you know

what you are worth, your own motivations, and what the recruiter wants (hey, you have the job ad in your hand), the recruiter on the other hand knows what he is looking for and knows your profile (hey, he has your resume on the table). Thus, the challenge is for you to convince the recruiter that you are the right person for the position and that that resume on the table meets the job description.

More and more recruiters are abandoning the traditional direct questions interview approach as they found out that direct questions do not lead to definite conclusions. Direct questions like "how would you react to angry customers?" are generally answered by the candidates in a theoretical manner and do not provide any idea on how they would react when facing real world situations. More, it is easy for the candidates to guess what the recruiter wants to verify from the question. They would then respond with answers prepared in advance. As a result, recruiters rely on their instincts to guess the future performance of their candidates.

Direct questions interviews have been thus replaced by a new type of interview: Behavioral interviews. These ones are based on the following principle: under the same circumstances and the same conditions, past behavior provides the best indication of future performance. They try to identify whether the candidate has the necessary skills (often called success factors) that are needed in the context of the proposed position. Independently of the success factors needed for the job, a recruiter's aim from an interview should be answering three main questions. These are:

- Can this person do the job? i.e. does he or she have the necessary skills, the knowledge, and the technical capabilities that are necessary to do the job? Does he or she have the general capabilities such as critical thinking?
- Is this person willing to do the job, i.e. willingness, motivation and optimism? It is important to note that the fact a person is capable of doing the job does not mean he will be willing to do it. More about this later.
- Will this person be able to fit in the organization and its culture? i.e. adaptation, compatibility with other employees, their thinking and views.

Your objective during the interview is to ensure that the answer to each of the above three questions is yes. Yes, you can do the job. Yes, you are willing and motivated to do the job and yes, you will fit in the organization culture and get along with your future colleagues.

The person who is looking to hire you is psychologically governed by fear. He is probably more fearful than you. He has deadlines to meet, budgets not to be exceeded, customers to satisfy, sales targets to hit and quality and security standards to respect... At the end of the day, it is his position that is in danger, and if he is organizing these interviews, it is probably because he needs to control this fear or eliminate it completely and for this he needs your help. Your role during the interview is to show him that you are the solution to his problems. You are the person on which he can rely to control and eliminate his fears.

Be careful of some recruiters who set up "fake" interviews with the hidden agenda of promoting and marketing their products and services. This practice is mainly used by consulting firms which instead of leaving their consultants on the bench during slow periods; they request them to interview candidates without the intention of hiring any. However, this practice is not widespread.

In all cases, whether it is an interview for a consulting firm, for a bank, for a start up, or even for a fast food restaurant, a competent recruiter should have clear unambiguous answers to these questions at the end the interview:

- Is the candidate mentally alert? Is he reactive?
- Is the candidate able to draw inferences and conduct logical reasoning to arrive at acceptable conclusions? Or is his thinking confused?
- Did the candidate follow a rational logic in planning his life and career so far?
- Is the candidate able to handle stress? Is he able to work under pressure?

Your objective during the interview is to score a maximum number of points responding to each of the above points. This book will explain to you step by step how to do this.

To Get Started

Your objective during the interview is to score a maximum number of points responding to each of the above points. This book will explain to you step by step how to do this.

Your interview will start when you say "hello" to the interviewer. This one will start scrutinizing your demeanor the first minute he identifies you in the corridor or the waiting room. He starts building a picture of you piece by piece. Don't hesitate to reach out and shake hands firmly. This will only show your charisma. Focus your attention on the interviewer. Avoid looking around the room, tapping your fingers, or other nervous movements.

You need to arrive 10 to 15 minutes before the interview. Sometimes, the candidates arrive exactly at the time of interview or even late, they don't have the time to collect their thoughts, they have their hands sweating when they shake the hand of the recruiter. They have the impression of being behind schedule and under pressure and they don't have the time to think and answer the questions correctly. They end up being hated by the recruiter.

Some recruiters start the interview with some chatting, some words about the weather, the day's news or sports. Although they do not mention your capabilities during this phase, don't forget that you are being evaluated. Recruiters are often trained on how to evaluate candidates using multiple criteria. They may be evaluating you communication skills in an informal setting. As a result, you should not limit yourself to smiles or to a yes or no. I have seen candidates who give a good idea of what being brain-dead looks like.

Don't go too far in the other direction and talk a lot. There is nothing worse than a candidate that talks and talks... The recruiter probably doesn't want to know the entire story of your life. Your responses should be concise and go directly to the point without any hesitation. Answer the questions simply without being too short. Indeed, it quickly becomes difficult to communicate with a person who answers questions in a word or two. I remember some interviews where trying to get an answer from the candidate was the equivalent of pulling his teeth. It was not pleasant. So, even if you are not the chatty type, you need to answer the questions completely and provide the best responses possible.

The Capability

for when it's your turn in the hot seat.

A huge part of the interview is based on probing and inferences. For example, most interviewers are savvy enough to know it is illegal to directly ask you about your age, but often you will get a question such as, "What year did you graduate from college?" that indirectly probes at your age. If you tell the truth, the interviewer then knows your age and may not want to hire you because of it. If you say you don't want to answer the question, you could come across poorly and may make the interviewer uncomfortable. Here is how you can finesse the situation. First, assume the interviewer does not have ulterior motives. Instead, figure that he or she is trying to learn something, albeit clumsily, about your ability to do the job. So listen to the question then ask your own question in return to determine the interviewer's underlying agenda.

For instance, you could respond, "I am curious to know why you are asking this. Are you worried that my skills might be out of date?" The interviewer should then respond with the reason for the question, which allows you to say something good about yourself. Frame your response as a showcase of what you have learned and prove that your training is current.

Other example: If the interviewer requests your career history, you might inquire, "Do you want me to start with my present situation or at the beginning?" This type of response demonstrates a candidate is preparing mentally for what's he's going to give to the recruiter. Pausing after you speak lets you collect your thoughts - and seek permission to continue. At the end of the answer you can resume by asking: "Did I answer your question enough? Do you want more examples? "

Probing is generally combined with the behavioral interview technique to test your general skills such as leadership and teamwork. For example, if the proposed position would require you to work in a team, his question may be: "Tell me of a case where you have coordinated a team? What did you do? What were the results?" He may even ask for a summary of the case before getting into the details. He may be trying to verify the truth of the case or identify some specific skills or weaknesses. He may ask questions like "what did you think at that time?", "why did he do that?", "Are you certain of this point?" It is critical that you answer these questions correctly as they are essential to your credibility.

Fortunately, there is a technique that allows you to do this correctly. It is called STAR. It is simply the most efficient technique in telling your behavior in a given situation where you used your general skills. The word STAR is a mnemonic to keep in mind the points that you need to mention when discussing the situation:

- *Situation:* Describe the situation in which you found yourself in.
- *Tasks:* Describe the tasks that you have

performed in that situation. You need to describe these tasks in a way that shows that you faced challenges and difficulties.

- *Actions:* Describe the actions you took in order overcome the challenges.
- *Results:* Describe the results of your actions. Present them in a positive way.

Here is an example illustrating how this technique is used:

The recruiter: Tell me of a situation where you have faced pressure?

You: I took over a project that was already running in 2 years delay with huge problems of quality. The customer has lost all faith in our capability of delivering and finalizing the project. Worst, he was threatening to stop it [situation]. My mission was to resolve all the problems of this project, with minimum cost, regain the trust of the customer and deliver the project within a year [Tasks]. At the time, our R&D and quality department were not cooperating. They were exchanging blames for the delays. I decided to create a single temporary that included the best resources from each department. This team objective was to resolve the problems one by one. The team held regular meetings with the customer, prioritized the problems, obtained the customer approval for the considered solutions, and then implemented these ones under my supervision [Actions]. At the end, we resolved all the problems in less than six months. The customer was very satisfied and even signed new projects with the company. The team that I created was disbanded and the company CEO put a new organization in place that is designed to foster cooperation between different departments [Results].

Some companies and particularly consulting firms use what is called "case studies" in order to evaluate the candidates' ability to perform their type of work. These case studies allow them to evaluate your problem resolution skills, your tolerance to ambiguous situation and your communication and interpersonal skills. They want to know whether you are able to identify, structure, approach and finally resolve a problem. They want to know if you are able to listen, articulate your thinking and reach conclusions without the help of others. As a result, the way you would approach the case is more important than the solution you reach. It is advised to think loudly so that the recruiter sees how you are thinking. Here is an example of the case:

The recruiter: In the following case, I will provide you some information about a case we have faced with one of our customers. I will ask you some questions to see how you would react if you were with us facing the same case. Remember, there are no "correct and wrong answers." I am just trying to see the process you would follow to resolve a problem.

First question: A large fast food chain has hired us to improve its profitability. You are going to have a first brainstorming session to identify different possible options for the customer. How would you proceed?

First answer: The recruiter tries to verify whether you are able to structure the problem. A good approach to the problem will be to mention the equation that gives the earnings of a commercial entity: earnings = revenues – cost, where revenues = price * quantity and cost = fixed cost + quantity* unit cost. In order for the chain to improve its profitability, the management can increase sales, and/or reduce cost.

Second question: You have mentioned two interesting ideas, can you provide more details?

Second answer: Ok, first let consider revenues, we need to ask the following questions: 1. can the chain increase prices without hurting sales? How its customers would react 2. Should we look to the revenues per outlet and try to increase this number, or should we consider the opening of new outlets? 3. Are there any creative solutions to increase revenues, like the launch of new products? Second, if we consider the second part of the equation (i.e. cost), we can consider the following questions: 1. Can the client reduce cost by selling the outlets buildings and then leasing them back? 2. Can he renegotiate the products and the ingredients he buys for the meals? 3. Can he reduce the cost of staff without impacting the quality of service provided to the customers?

Third question: The customer market is very competitive and is thus price sensible. The fixed costs are stable. You should consider the reduction of variable cost. More precisely, the customer wants to reduce the cost of the goods he purchases (like these of meat, bread, vegetables and sauces). Without knowing too much on the situation, what can you propose as solutions to reduce this cost? What are the solutions that look more attractive to you and why?

Third answer: The purchased products can be divided in two different categories: food and packaging. Regarding the food, the customer can renegotiate his contracts with its suppliers; he can also look for cheaper ingredients or reduce the quantity of the ingredients in his products. However, these two last solutions are risky propositions and may impact the reputation of the customer. For the packaging, the customer may renegotiate his contracts with his suppliers or search for cheaper alternatives.

Fourth question: The client has indeed successfully renegotiated his contracts with his suppliers two years ago and obtained lower prices. So he is looking for other solutions to further reduce the cost of the purchases.

Fourth answer: Here are some questions that the client may consider: 1. Can he reduce the size of the packages? 2. Can he reduce the thickness of the packages while still protecting food? 3. Can he charge for the ketchup and the sauces? 4. Can he reduce the number of paper towels he gives to customers?

The Willingness

Through the answers of the previous chapter, you have demonstrated to the recruiter that you are capable of accomplishing the required work. Through the questions of this chapter, the recruiter will try to verify that you will be willing to do the work. "But is there a candidate who can do the job but is not willing to do it?" You would ask me. The answer to this question is yes. You should consider all these fifty-something jobless people to understand that. They have the technical skills, they have the general skills, but they are seen as de-motivated, not willing to go the extra mile for the company. They give the impression that they are sitting there, unconcerned, waiting for their retirement.

In one of my interviews as a recruiter, I saw a 40 year old woman, who was facing a huge dilemma when her son of 10 years insisted on choosing soccer as his sport. The issue was that the municipality had a rugby club, not soccer. So instead of convincing her son of changing his passion and practicing rugby, she opted for the most difficult option. She wrote to the mayor, mobilized other children's parents, looked for financing from the soccer national association and succeeded in creating a soccer club at the municipality so that her son can practice his hobby. This woman was looking for an assistant position and she got it. It is this type of behavior, this determination and this initiative taking spirit that recruiters are looking for.

Another example, during a candidate's interview, I asked him if he was ready to cancel his holidays to work on an urgent project. To my surprise, his answer was negative. This person was looking for a career, maybe a lifetime career in the company, but was not ready to sacrifice two weeks of his time for this career. Needless to say that he was rejected. At the end of the interview, I was even wondering whether it was me who was abnormal or whether we were living in different times.

How can I demonstrate my willingness? It is not necessary to show it because it shows up naturally. Somebody who spends his free time developing software programs and a websites is probably very motivated to do an IT job. In fact, willingness shows naturally in a resume. Unfortunately, it also shows the lack of it. This is shown in what we call zigzagging resumes. It is not difficult to find candidates without any coherency in their career path. They have probably obtained a bachelor degree in chemistry, but then decided that chemistry was not made for them, decided to follow a master degree in history, and finally here they are, applying for a position in marketing. How would a candidate with this path explain his passion for marketing? He would not be credible.

Finally, there is a last question that allows the recruiter to evaluate your willingness. At a given time in the selection process, this question will be raised. This question is not a signal. The fact that the recruiter asks you this question does not mean that you are selected for the position. Similarly, if this question has not been asked, it does not mean that you are being rejected. There are no exact answers to this question. Here also, you should do your home work and know what your worth is on the job market. This can be done by asking friends in the same business about their salaries or checking the internet and magazines. In all cases, the most recommended answer is the following: "Indeed, the salary is important, but it is not my primary concern. My main motivation is the nature of the work offered in this position which looks exciting from what you have described to me. Now, if you ask me, if I am looking for something fair and in comparison with my other colleagues who have the same profile, I think x dollars would be reasonable. At that moment, the recruiter would either write down the number and move to something else or start negotiating and bargaining. Don't negotiate. You are here for a career not dollars. Simply ask that the recruiter makes his best offer and tell him that you would consider it.

Be careful not to go too far and sell yourself cheaply. For example, it may be tempting to offer to work temporarily for free or to take a lesser salary than what a job pays. But experts say such bold moves often backfire on candidates. Employers want value, they don't want cheap. You can try turning the tables by asking interviewers what the company has budgeted for the position.

In some cases, you may be looking just for a job to get you through so you might consider a less-than-perfect fit. But if you aren't really excited about an opportunity, keep it to yourself and interview like it is the job that is first on your list of preferences. Nobody wants to hire someone who's going to run for the door when times get better.

No matter how you're feeling, keep your personal feelings out of the interview process. Instead, always exude an upbeat attitude. For example, if you were laid off, instead of lamenting the situation, you might say the experience prompted you to reassess your skills, and that's what led you here.

However, some try hard to show a fit between their profiles and the proposed position even if there is no interest. They like to say that their profiles are not typical thinking and that this is a plus. However the truth is totally different. In my opinion, there are no atypical profiles. They are simply a justification for erratic career paths. The number of people who have the luxury to say that they have atypical career paths is very limited. These are exceptional people who can make U turns in their careers and their lives without having to explain it. They are the Arnold Schwarzenegger's and Ronald Reagan's of this world. More, even if some use this phrase, there is always some logic in their careers and their lives. It is this logic that you should stress during the interview.

In all cases, there is only a limited number of profiles in this world. If the recruiter is looking for an IT specialist, he would be expecting an IT education (a bachelor degree or a master degree in technology), internships in IT or around IT, skills in programming, operating systems, may be networking and databases and may some DIY applications.

Similarly, if the recruiter is looking for a biologist, he would be expecting somebody with a degree in biology, with an internship in some biology laboratories, and some scientific research. He or she knows something about chemistry and has probably published some scientific articles in international reviews.

There is a huge difference between somebody who has changed employers four times over the last 10 years, who did two engagements abroad, followed an evening class in his/her area of expertise along with some months at university and another person who spent his last 10 years in the same company doing the same job. The first will be able to say that his profile is atypical. The second cannot. But now with the globalization of the world economy and the job market, everyone is looking to have an atypical profile which is in high demand by recruiters. Indeed, now it is the second profile that has became atypical in a negative way.

No matter how good your skills are on paper, your actions, your behavior, the way you dress, the way you speak and you project yourself, what you say and what you don't say, all this is evaluated and weighted when the recruiter considers the decision to hire you. When you hear recruiters speaking about how they conduct their interviews, you will have the impression that they are picky and give a ton of reasons to explain why they have rejected a candidate. But this is human nature. No recruiter likes the guilt of rejecting a candidate that later turned out to be brilliant at a competing company. So to reject a candidate, they don't need one small reason (nobody has ever refused Cindy Crawford because she has a beauty spot), instead they need multiple reasons that add up to each other to give a highly negative impression about the candidate.

Then, you would tell me the risk for the recruiter of hiring a candidate that is found later to be a low performer is bigger and more serious than the risk of rejecting a candidate that is in fact a high performer (something like drugs when they get approved, where it is possible to reject a drug that turns out to be safe while approving a harmful drug should be avoided at any price). After all, the recruiter will have to fire a low performer with lengthy and expensive procedures.

The answer to this question is already in the selection process itself. It is for this reason that there are multiple candidates for the same opening. It is for this reason that the recruiter proceeds by successive eliminations. He has a list of candidates that are, on paper, capable, qualified and willing. He is not searching directly for the best candidate; he is looking to eliminate the not so good ones to keep the best candidates for the end.

Here are examples of several small details that have led to a global negative impression about the candidate:

- An HR director summarized his impression about a candidate for a senior management position by saying: "He made me wait several minutes while he was finishing a phone call at the lobby, did not recognize me despite the fact that I interviewed him before, and he behaved in an arrogant way throughout the selection process". It was obvious that this candidate was not a good fit for our organization.

- I interviewed one candidate who initially seemed to be perfect for the proposed position. He was even recommended by the CEO of the company; his industry experience was wide and far reaching; his rolodex was priceless; his resume included an impressive list of deals he helped broker around the world. The problem is that he was so confident that he did not ask any questions to me or to other interviewers.

He did not want to know their roles, their views and the way he could work and cooperate with them. He left the impression that he was not interested by the company or his future colleagues. It was clear that he was not motivated, and it was not serious for him if he didnot get the job. And indeed, he did not get it. I told myself, "This person has a strong etiquette and judgment problem". My advice is that when you are going to interview for a job, interview 100%, and put everything else out of your mind.

- I interviewed a candidate who was swearing like crazy; he used language that was not up to the standards of the proposed executive position. If your mother has always told you to sit up straight, to avoid putting elbows on the table, and to watch your language, it is certainly for a reason. She knew that others will judge you based on your behavior. Candidates who are not careful of their behavior always fall in this trap, and destroy their chances of joining the company of their dreams.

- When I asked the CEO of a company why he rejected a candidate for a sales position, his response was as follow: "his shirt was not ironed. It looked like he wore it the previous day, threw it somewhere in his room and then reused it for the interview day. He did not even try to hide it with a jacket. I thought if he did not take the time to impress me at our first encounter, how would he do in front of very demanding customers?"

"Dress for Success" was the title of a very popular book from the seventies, and even if the dress code has been relaxed, especially at IT startups, there is no excuse for dressing with non ironed shirts, or wearing tight T-shirts, or ties with traces of coffee. Serious candidates know that the best way to enhance their chances of getting the job is to look professional and make a good first impression.

In case where you are asking yourself, why you did not get an offer following the last interview despite the fact that you have the necessary qualifications and skills, you probably need to look at the impression you gave to the recruiter. This impression speaks more than words.

The Fit

The work environment is sensible. It is the place, after your home, where you spend most of your time. Recruiters don't want somebody who may destroy this fragile environment. They don't want somebody who will not be able to fit in their company. My experience shows that the best way to show your capacity to fit in can be done by showing you capacity to tell stories. Yes, you read it right: Telling stories. Recruiters, like children, like story tellers.

Recruiters don't want boring people. I know somebody with whom I worked for three years. And during that long period, he never, not even once, told me an interesting story. Even if he had been raped by some aliens, or chased by a terminator, or lost a million dollars in a casino, he always ends up messing his story and destroying it. Quickly, you fall sleeping listening to him. Unfortunately he has not been raped by an alien, has never been chased by a terminator and has never been in a casino. All what happened in his life over the previous week was the fact that he bought a newspaper. And without surprise, he thought this event was important enough to make a conversation out of it. Honestly, at one time during the conversation, I thought I was going to kill him.

I have the sincere conviction that the best quality a human can have, is not his beauty, his intelligence or his fortune. It is his ability to tell stories in way that makes them intriguing, live and exciting. His knowledge of what should be included, what should not be told and what should be twisted to infuse a soul to the story. If you don't have this ability, you should probably keep silent. Don't say anything.

As a general advice, always watch the interviewer's body language for hints that your answers are getting boring. He may stop taking notes, check his watch or glance at his computer. He may even cut you off to refocus the interview if he notices your story is getting boring or sees you talking about extraneous issues, such as your personal life.

Recruiters have even invented a test for this, the "airport" test. Suppose you are with a colleague at an airport on your way back after having met a customer, suddenly you learn that your flight has been delayed by 3 hours and you angrily cancel the family dinner you have planned. Now, you have 3 hours of time to kill passing them with your colleague. Now, imagine that that colleague is that candidate in front of you.

So when the recruiter asks a question about a situation when you faced a specific challenge (cf.

chapter capability), you should respond with a story. Although it is unlikely you have a story that fits every conceivable query, the task of preparing becomes easier when you realize that interviewers typically are interested in only five or six general categories. Instead of trying to be ready for every potential question, come up with stories to fit these general issues, such as how you handled conflict, pressure or ethics. It may help to think of each issue as a bucket and mentally place a story or two in each one. Be generic in your approach, and when asked a question along one of those lines, you can move to the story you have in one of those buckets.

When the recruiter asks the question "have you any questions for me", it is very important that you have questions ready. "I don't have any" is definitely not the right response. Dr. C. Randall Powell, the author of Career Planning Today, proposes excellent strategies to handle this point. Basically, the questions should incite the recruiter to react positively. Also, the questions should show that you are interested in knowing more about the organization. By choosing intelligent and serious questions, you show that you are serious about considering a career in the company.

Finally, in order to evaluate your fit, the recruiter may ask you some surprising questions. You should expect that and avoid being surprised or shocked. Often, these questions are designed for the single purpose of testing your reaction. Examples of such questions can be: "tell me a joke" or "in which period of history would you have preferred to live". These questions cannot be prepared in advance. The interviewer objective is to force you to react in an expected situation. The best advice for this situation is to think and respond naturally. Avoid anything in relation to gender, religion or race.

Whatever the responses you give, this is always about marketing yourself without going too far. Self marketing is as important for a job hunter as air is for a human. In order to survive and live, a man human needs air the second he is born. Similarly, as soon as you start considering a first job or a new job, you need to put yourself in a marketing process; you need to literally sell yourself to all the people who want to listen. You need to do it. You need to overcome your shyness. Show the extravert side of your personality to increase your chances of getting that job quickly.

Post-Interview Tasks

The interview is not over until you have walked out the door. The conclusion of the interview which generally lasts from 5 to 10 minutes is very important because this is when the recruiter evaluates your global performance. Stay positive and concentrated. The interview ends when the interviewer stands up. It is at that time that you should stand up, shake the recruiters hand and thank him for his consideration. Now the decision is his.

In most cases, you know whether you did well or not. Sometimes, you did well, very well but then you start thinking about the points where you could better. You start telling yourself, "I could have said this... I should not have said that".

In all cases, know that there is a last chance for you to stay in touch with recruiter. In fact, you should use this chance systematically and independently from the level of your performance during the interview. It is called the "thank you letter" and it has three objectives:

- Remind the recruiter that you are here and still alive. If you are the only one to send the letter, this will give you an advantage in comparison with other candidates. Also, the simple fact that the recruiter needs to file the letter will oblige him to search for your application and see it again. In the worst case scenario, if it is his secretary that would receive the letter and file it, she may leave your application on top of the pile, on top of others' applications.

- Thank the recruiter (with courtesy you always win points and lose none) and remind him that you are still interested by the proposed position and that you appreciated what you have seen and heard during the interview or the company visit.

- Finally, and this is may be the most important, add complementary information to your application. Reformulate and stress the points that were not discussed enough during the interview. Use the letter also to provide updates about your situation (you have obtained your degree or succeeded in obtaining the CFA certification after the interview for example). All these positive updates may trigger a positive reaction from the recruiter.

Here is an example of a thank you letter:

Brian Wilkinson

"I was delighted to meet you and discuss the career opportunities offered by Auto Systems. I am very impressed by the innovative solutions you are developing and I renew my interest in joining your team and participating in your projects.

As discussed during our interview, I have spent my last two years working on the development of real time systems for automobiles. With this experience and my passion for real time applications, I am convinced that I will be able to bring real value to Auto Systems.

I thank you for your time and remain available for any additional information regarding my experience and my motivation."

Sometimes, instead of a single interview, you may have spent the entire day interviewing with different people from the company and even got to lunch with one of them. In this case, should you send an individual letter to each interviewer or a single grouped letter? There is no straightforward answer to this question; you need to choose your approach according to the organization of the company. If the interviews you did with these different people look similar (with the same questions and the same issues), it is highly likely that these people work in the same department. In this case, it is better to send a single letter. In the opposite case, it would be better to send out an individual letter to each interviewer even if this takes more time to prepare. Also look closely for spelling and grammatical errors. In a competitive job market, employers have the luxury of choice, and even a minor faux pas can hurt your chances.

Also, don't stalk the interviewer. Wait at least a week before checking on your candidacy. Call recruiters only at their office, even if their business card lists a cell number. Leave a message if you get voicemail. These days, recruiters typically have caller ID and can tell if you've tried reaching them multiple times without leaving a voicemail. There is always a fine line between enthusiasm and over-enthusiasm.

Finally, even if you have completely failed the interview, don't take it personally. I have never met somebody in this world who did not fail at least one interview. If this happens, think that the position was probably not made for you (there was not a fit between your profile and the job description). Learn from this experience and move on to the next opportunity.

Pre-Interview Checklist

This chapter is a checklist of 6 points that need to be verified before proceeding to an interview. They are necessary for a successful interview.

Did you do your home work about the company?

You need to learn about the products and services provided by the company. You need to learn about its executive committee, its board, its projects, its competitors and its culture. Also, you need to keep in mind the qualifications needed for the proposed position, even if this may be difficult for a cold application. At the end of your companies search, you should be able to explain why your profile is in line with the employer's needs and why you should be, in theory, the best candidate for the job.

Practice, practice, practice,...

You will notice that your presentation and

performance will increase with more interviews. In order to avoid failing interviews because of lack of preparation, it is recommended to perform simulated interviews with friends and family members. Always keep in mind the three or four unique selling points that you should focus on during an interview. These points should be always in relation with the needs of the company. For example if this one is doing business with Latin America, your Spanish language skills become a selling point while they are not if the company is doing most of its business with Asia.

During one of my interviews, I told to a recruiter the summary of the most important events that his company faced over the last 10 years. He was so surprised that he thought I have previously worked from the company, started rereading my resume, then gave up and simply asked me the question: "How do you know all this?" It was not a secret, I researched the company on the internet and after an hour of home work, I got a fairly detailed idea about the company and how it evolved over the previous decade.

Another example: I was interviewing candidates for a manufacturing company and was impressed by the preparedness of a candidate. He knew the company's product line and what markets it was already in. He clearly and effectively explained how he could cut costs, increase sales and expand market share based on what he'd done in his current job. The candidate was hired.

Be ready to discuss any weakness that may reduce your chances

You need to always be positive and avoid searching for excuses for yourself. Instead of attracting the attention of the recruiter on your weaknesses, focus on the strategy and the process you have put in place in order to reduce or completely eliminate these weaknesses. You can also use the interview to focus on some of your profile positive attributes that have not been neglected or not discussed so far during the interview. For example, it is possible to have an average GPA if in the time of your studies you worked part time to pay for your studies and be financially independent.

Do you have the necessary equipment for the interview?

Whether you are a male or a female, dress in business attire. Men should wear a suit with a tie. Some exceptions still persist when it comes to marketing agencies when for creativity reasons, semi-casual attire is acceptable. We used to say that the state of somebody shoes gives a fair idea about the wearer. So you need to be careful to the state of your shoes and make sure these are well polished. Minimize the number of jewelries or the power of perfumes.

Did you take additional copies of your resume with you?

The recruiter may forget or lose your resume in a pile of documents. Always take backup copies of your resume to the interview.

Do you know the place where the interview will take place?

You need to arrive 10 to 15 minutes before the interview. This will give you enough time to organize your thoughts. You will be surprised of the advantages this will bring to you in comparison with other candidates who arrive at the last minute. Also you can use these 10 minutes to have some hints about the company and assess whether you would like to work in this place. In order to avoid being late, you may visit the place the previous day to find the address and how to get there.

If you have checked all the previous points, you are ready to proceed with the interview.

Mistakes to be avoided

Neglect preparation

Not being able to respond to the question: "what do you know about our company?" may simply be the end to your interview. Information related to the company history, organization, mission and objectives are generally available on the companies' websites. These need to be read and reviewed. You can also print them and reread them just before the interview to keep them fresh in your memory.

Poor communication

It is important that you communicate well with all the people you meet during your hunt for a job. But the most important is that you connect positively with the recruiter. Shake hands, don't avoid eye contact, show assurance, look for answers to your questions and show to the recruiter that you are the right candidate for the position even before answering the first question.

Avoid distractions

I got the case of a candidate (who by the way was not selected for the position), who did not hesitate to answer his phone in the middle of the interview. Switch off your phone. Also, avoid bringing in coffee, food and any other distraction. There should be only

you, your resume, application forms (if any) and the
list of your references.

Self entitlement

An overblown sense of entitlement can lead to
a variety of candidate misbehaviors (peeking at
blackberries, insulting the receptionists, using the
company meeting rooms for meeting calls...) that
will kill your chances. The solution: Always act like
a guest from the time you enter the company to the
time you leave it.

Confusing information

Even if you have sent you resume, and have
copies of it in hand, the recruiter may ask you fill in
an application form (because this is the rule in his
company). In this case, be sure that the information
you indicate in the form is in line with your resume
and is correct. This includes the dates of previous
positions, the dates of degrees and certifications.

Giving a wrong answer

Make sure that you have understood the question
and took the time to think about what the recruiter
wants to verify before answering. You can be rejected
due simply to a wrong answer as in the following

situation: The recruiter described in a detailed manner a marketing and sales position. He mentioned that cold calls and prospection were part of the job. The candidate responds by indicating what he likes and what he does not like in sales and marketing and using the following words: "what I don't like in the use of cold calls, is that it is difficult, the results are never there" This response showed a lake of motivation and the candidate was rejected.

Dispraise previous experiences

Your previous manager was an idiot. All your colleagues from your previous job were stupid. You hated your previous job and you could not wait to leave. Even if all this was true, you should not say it. In an interview, I heard a candidate insulting the company he used to work for. The problem is that same company was one of our main customers. It was unthinkable to hire this candidate with such negative opinion about our main customer. It would have been the source of major trouble in the future.

The world in which we live is smaller than what we think. And it is even smaller if you are a working in a highly specialized niche industry. You cannot know what the recruiter knows or does not know, even about your previous employer which you believe is an idiot... Similarly, you don't want the recruiter to think that one day you may speak about him and his company in the same way.

Maintain the right amount of eye contact

Using too little or too much eye contact can impact a recruiter's perception of you. If you avoid eye contact after being asked a question, or you look down, it can suggest dishonesty. Many candidates look to the right or left of the interviewer or out the windows instead of making eye contact which can indicate disinterest or lack of confidence. A good approach to show a recruiter you are interested is to alternate looking at their eyes, mouth and shoulders.

However, be careful not to overdo the eye contact. Some candidates concentrate on maintaining eye contact too much and create a feeling of uneasiness to the recruiter.

Fidgeting

Fidgeting is a telltale sign of nerves, and although many recruiters make allowances for nervousness, they will also expect you to handle pressure with ease if you're seeking a high-level job. If you display your nerves too much during an interview, you may be at a disadvantage. Aside from displaying your nervousness, fidgeting is annoying and distracting to recruiters and although everyone has their own personal fidgets (like touching your hair for example), the key is to control them during interviews so they don't distract your interviewer. To keep yourself from fidgeting, bring a prop, such as a pen and pad, to keep your hands occupied.

Be conscious of posture while standing and sitting

Slouching, whether you are standing to greet the interviewer or sitting down, suggests a lack of self esteem. During an interview you should appear confident and engaged in the conversation and poor posture can send a message that you are indifferent or too casual. Sit up with your backside at the very back of the chair which will create a slight lean forward position that shows interest and engagement in the conversation. Remember to keep your shoulders back.

Avoid "closed" body language

Body language such as crossed arms and clenched fists show defensiveness and tension. They are physically closed positions and suggest that the candidate doesn't want to open up. Women tend to cross their arms when they are cold. It is recommended to dress warmly if you tend to get cold so you don't inadvertently send the wrong message. Sit with your ankles crossed or feet flat on the floor and use open hand gestures which suggest friendliness.

Avoid too much self-promotion

Like many contestants on some singing reality TV show who extol the greatness of their singing abilities and then end up sent home, some candidates sing praises about their abilities without delivering tangible evidence to back up the claims. This particularly true in tough economic conditions where, out of desperation, many candidates convince themselves they're qualified for positions that don't match their profiles and they want to try anything and everything. By trying to sell themselves hard, they end up losing credibility.

Index

A

Actions 24
articulate 25
assessment 21
assessment tests 21

B

Behavioral interviews 10
body language 65

C

caller ID 52
Capability 19
case studies 25
checklist 21
communication 61
critical thinking 11

D

Dispraise 63
distractions 61
Dress 39

E

eye contact 64

F

Fidgeting 64
Fit 41

G

global 9

I